Discovering Science

SEASONS

Rebecca Hunter

RAINTREE
STECK-VAUGHN
PUBLISHERS

A Harcourt Company

Austin   New York
www.steck-vaughn.com

Published by Raintree Steck-Vaughn Publishers, an imprint of Steck-Vaughn Company

Acknowledgments
Project Editors: Rebecca Hunter, Pam Wells
Illustrated by Pamela Goodchild, Stefan Chabluk, and Keith Williams
Designed by Ian Winton

Planned and produced by Discovery Books

Library of Congress Cataloging-in-Publication Data
Hunter, Rebecca (Rebecca K. de C.)
Seasons / Rebecca Hunter.
p. cm. — (Discovering science)
Includes bibliographical references and index.
ISBN 0-7398-3247-6
1. Seasons--Juvenile literature. [1. Seasons.] I. Title

QB 637.4 .H86 2001
508.2--dc21   00-042459

1 2 3 4 5 6 7 8 9 0 BNG 05 04 03 02 01
Printed and bound in the United States of America.

Note to the reader: You will find difficult words in the glossary on page 30.

CONTENTS

SIGNS OF THE SEASONS

Have you noticed how certain things happen at a particular time of year? Birds lay their eggs in spring. Butterflies appear in summer. In autumn the leaves on some trees turn yellow and gold and fall to the ground. In winter it turns colder and snow may fall.

All these events are signs of different seasons. A season is a time of year that has a particular kind of weather. The changes in the seasons affect all types of plants and animals, and humans too.

▲ *A blue titmouse feeding its young.*

REASONS FOR SEASONS

Seasons are caused by the way Earth moves around, or orbits, the Sun. It takes 365 days and 6 hours for Earth to orbit the Sun. Because of the way Earth is tilted, one half receives more sunlight than the other for half the year. When the Northern Hemisphere, the northern half of Earth, is tilted toward the Sun, it will have long, sunny days. The countries there will be having summer.

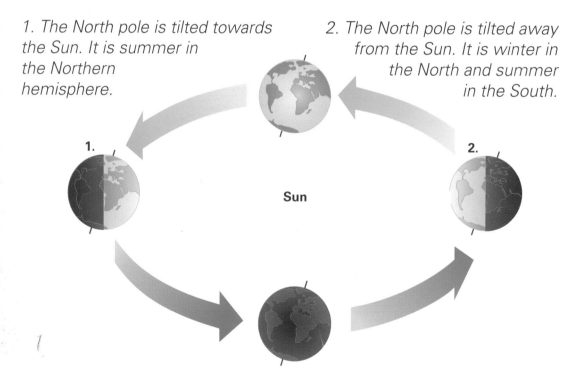

1. The North pole is tilted towards the Sun. It is summer in the Northern hemisphere.

2. The North pole is tilted away from the Sun. It is winter in the North and summer in the South.

Sun

At the same time, the Southern Hemisphere will be having short winter days because it is tilted away from the Sun. Six months later, when Earth is on the other side of the Sun, the seasons will have swapped.
It will be summer in the south and winter in the north. In between summer and winter, the hemispheres will have autumn or spring.

The seasons are very different in different parts of the world. When you look at a map of the world, you will see an imaginary line in the middle called the equator. To the north and south of the equator are two more imaginary lines called the Tropic of Cancer and the Tropic of Capricorn.

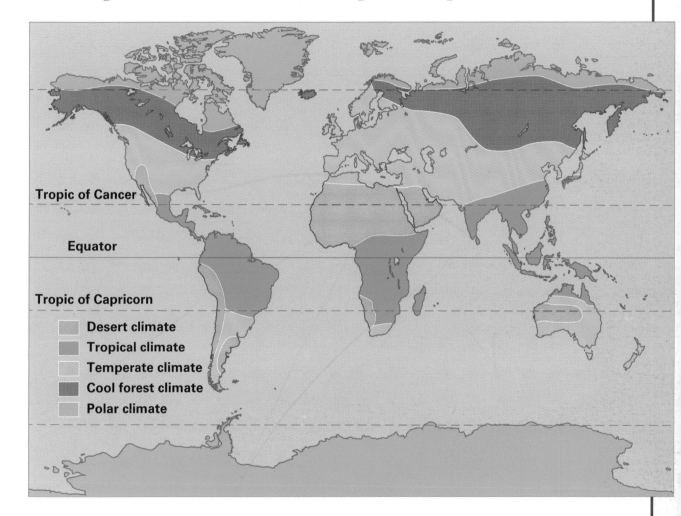

Tropic of Cancer

Equator

Tropic of Capricorn

- Desert climate
- Tropical climate
- Temperate climate
- Cool forest climate
- Polar climate

The area between these two lines is known as the tropics. The weather here is always hot. At the extreme north and south of Earth are the polar regions. Polar climates are cold and dry. The area between the tropics and the polar regions is called the temperate zone. Temperate regions have warm summers and cold winters.

TROPICAL SEASONS

Because of the shape of Earth, the land in the tropics receives more sunlight than the land at the poles.

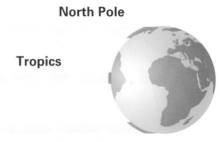

North Pole

Tropics

South Pole

Countries in the tropics have hot or warm weather all year. The seasons are not different from one another in temperature changes. But they differ in rainfall. Seasons in the tropics are either wet or dry.

POLAR SEASONS

The poles have only two seasons. Six months of summer and six months of winter. Polar seasons are very extreme. In winter at the South Pole, the Sun does not rise at all for several months. At the same time it is summer at the North Pole. In countries such as Finland, there is daylight for 24 hours a day in summer. Polar areas are called the "lands of the midnight Sun."

TEMPERATE SEASONS

Between the poles and the tropics are the temperate zones. There are four different seasons: spring, summer, autumn, and winter. The farther away from the equator you go, the more the seasons become apparent. Maine has much colder winters than Florida, where it remains warm all winter.

This picture shows the movement of the Sun throughout one day in Norway in mid-summer. Over 24 hours the Sun does not set at all.

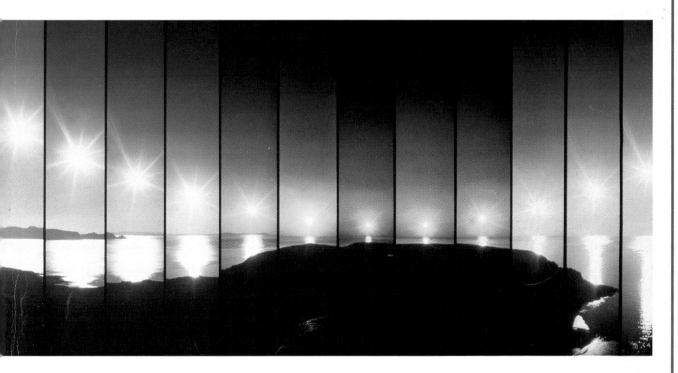

SPRING

In spring the days begin to get longer and the weather starts to get warmer. After the short, cold winter days, everyone enjoys seeing the sunshine again and the animals and plants start to wake up.

SPRING GROWTH

Many plants stop growing in winter. Spring is the time everything starts to grow again. Root tips grow longer and push their way through the soil. Buds on the trees get ready to burst into new green leaves.

Seeds, left behind from last year, start to grow, and spring flowers shoot up from bulbs. The bulb is a store of food that helps the plant grow until its leaves appear.

Daffodils are spring flowers that grow from bulbs.

PROJECT

Grow your own seedlings

You will need

Sunflower seeds
A small watering can
Notebook and pencil
Pots
Compost
Water
A tape measure and a ruler

1. Fill each pot with compost.

2. Plant a seed in each pot and water it. Leave the pots in a sunny position.

3. Water the pots every day and check for signs of growth.

4. When the seeds start to grow you can measure them each day.

5. Keep a record of their growth.

ANIMALS IN SPRING

For many animals winter is a hard time with cold temperatures and little food. In spring the temperatures are warmer, and life becomes easier.

A tiger swallowtail butterfly on oxeye daisies.

The growth of new plants means there is more food available for animals. Bees, beetles, and butterflies are some of the insects that eat more of this food and start to breed in spring.

Insects provide food for other animals. Many birds have migrated, or moved to another region or climate, to escape the winter weather. They return for the summer to eat from the new supply of insects. The golden plover spends the winter 15,000 miles away in Argentina. Then it returns in spring to the tundra of North America.

In spring birds begin to make their nests. Sometimes they choose unusual spots for nests.

This great gray owl is nesting on a tree stump.

PROJECT

Raise your own butterflies

You will need
A large jar with holes in the lid
Some butterfly caterpillars
Tissue paper

> **Don't touch caterpillars; some can give you a bad rash.**

1. Check the leaves of plants, bushes, and trees for caterpillars. Oak trees and cabbage leaves are good places to look.

2. Put your caterpillars in the jar with a layer of damp tissue paper in the bottom. Keep this paper damp, but not wet.

3. Make sure you collect leaves from the plant you found these insects on. Use these leaves to feed the caterpillars. If you don't feed them the right food, they will die.

4. When each caterpillar is fully grown, it attaches itself to a twig. Then its skin hardens into a pupa.

5. It will stay like this for several weeks until the caterpillar has changed into a butterfly.

6. In the end, the pupa case will split, and the adult butterfly will crawl out.

7. You will be able to find out what kind of butterfly it is. Look it up in a book on butterflies. Then let it fly away.

SUMMER

Summer is the hottest season of the year. The Sun rises earlier and sets later in summer, so the days are long and warm. Plants are full of leaves in summer. Parks, yards, and rural areas all turn green.

PHOTOSYNTHESIS

Light energy from the Sun

Plant growth

Water is taken in from the roots

PHOTOSYNTHESIS

Green plants need sunlight to grow. Their green leaves capture the energy in sunlight and turn it into sugars. The plant uses the sugar for growth. We call this process photosynthesis.

Water moves through a plant all the time. It is drawn in by the roots and passes out again through the leaves. You can prove this by doing an experiment.

PROJECT

Collecting water from plants

You will need
A leafy tree or shrub
Two large plastic bags
Some string

1. On a dry day, tie a plastic bag over some leaves on a tree. If you can find a twig with no leaves on it, tie another bag over this as well.

2. Come back after a few hours. The bag over the leaves should have collected some moisture in it. The other bag will be dry.

3. You have collected the water from just a few leaves. Imagine how much water a whole forest of trees would give off.

TREE-MENDOUS!
An average-sized tree will take as much as 50 buckets of water out of the ground on a hot day.

FLOWERS

As well as producing green leaves, many plants flower in summer. Flowers produce the seeds of a plant, but first they also need pollen. Pollination, or getting pollen, takes place when pollen from one flower is taken to another flower of the same kind. Insects, such as bees and butterflies, and some birds help by carrying pollen from one flower to another. They are attracted to the flowers by their bright colors and sweet scents.

A bee collecting nectar from a common toadflax flower.

Summer is the time of a good food supply for animals. They make use of the extra food to fatten themselves and to feed their young.

CHANGING COLORS

Some animals change color with the seasons. The Arctic hare and Arctic fox have white fur in winter to keep them well hidden in the snow. When summer comes, and the snow melts, they shed their coats. They grow a new brown summer coat to match the soil and shrubs.

▼ *An Arctic fox in its winter coat.*

Autumn

Autumn is also called the "fall." It is easy to understand why. One of the first signs of autumn is that the leaves on the trees turn yellow, orange, or brown and fall to the ground. In autumn the days get cooler and shorter, and plants and animals sense that winter is coming.

Colorful autumn forests in the Wasatch Mountains in Utah.

Seeds

Autumn is the time for plants to shed their seeds. Seeds are spread around in different ways. Some seeds are inside a covering called a fruit. Some fruits, such as berries, are soft and juicy and good to eat. Birds and animals eat the fruit, spreading the seeds around in their droppings.

Some trees, such as the ash, box elder, red and sugar maple, have seeds with wings. The wind makes these seeds fly like helicopters and carries them far away.

PROJECT

Flying seeds

You will need
A collection of different kinds of seeds with wings
A chair
A tape measure
A friend

1. Take your seeds into your backyard or a park.

2. Have a friend hold the chair. Stand on it. Throw the seeds into the air, one at a time.

3. Notice how the seeds fly and how far.

4. Measure the distance each seed falls and record it on a chart below.

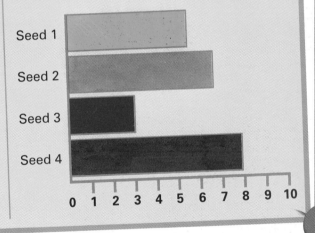

5. Which type of seed flew farthest?

Seed 1	
Seed 2	
Seed 3	
Seed 4	

0 1 2 3 4 5 6 7 8 9 10

Evergreen trees have fruits called cones. It takes two years for most cones to grow fully and for their seeds to ripen. The cones will only open and shed their seeds in dry weather. If you find a closed cone on the ground, bring it inside and put it in a warm place. In time it will open, and you will see the seeds inside.

PREPARING FOR WINTER

In autumn, animals start to get ready for winter. Most animals need to find ways to store food for the cold months ahead. All summer they have been getting ready for winter by eating well and storing extra fat in their bodies.

Some animals and birds collect and hide food. Squirrels race around in autumn hiding nuts. They will not remember where they have hidden them all. So without knowing it, they have helped plant many new trees.

The acorn woodpecker pecks holes in a tree and uses them to store acorns.

MIGRATION AND HIBERNATION

Animals that cannot survive in the cold have two choices. They can either migrate to warmer areas, or hibernate to avoid the cold weather. Birds find it easier to migrate. Flying gets them out of the area quickly, although the distances they travel can be huge. The Arctic tern travels 24,856 miles (40,000 km) from the Arctic to the Antarctic each year.

Hibernating animals slow down their body processes, so that the body is only just alive. True hibernators remain inactive all winter, because they would lose too much energy if they woke up.

WINTER

Everything seems to slow down in winter. The days get shorter and the temperatures fall. Plants stop growing. Many trees look dead without their leaves.

Winter weather is much colder. If the temperatures drop below freezing, frosts may occur in the early mornings. Snow and sleet may fall. Ice and freezing rain are part of winter, too.

STAYING WARM

Many birds and other animals disappear from the countryside when they either migrate away or go into hibernation. Small animals, such as squirrels and chipmunks, look for piles of leaves and stalks to hibernate in. As the plant life slowly breaks down, it gives off heat. This heat keeps the temperature from dropping below freezing. So the animals stay warm.

The animals that remain active in winter have to find ways of keeping themselves warm. Thick fur is essential to animals that are going to live through a snowy winter.

A fox has a thick coat that keeps it warm in winter.

FINDING FOOD

Wild animals find it difficult to get enough food in winter. Plants are not growing and the ground may be covered with snow.

You can help the birds in your area live through winter by giving them food and, in some places, water. Don't start this project unless you are prepared to do it all winter since the birds will depend on you. They may suffer if you suddenly stop feeding them.

PROJECT

Make a bird feeder

You will need
An empty plastic bottle
A large bag of shelled, unsalted peanuts
Some strong string
2 or 3 sticks of wood
A sharp knife or pair of scissors

1. Ask an adult to help you cut some slits in the bottle. The slits should start in the middle and run to the top or bottom.

2. Push the sticks through the slits, so the birds will have something to perch on.

3. Fill the bottle with nuts and put the top on. Make two holes in the bottom of the bottle. Thread the string through the holes to hang the feeder.

4. Hang the bottle from a strong branch.

5. Keep the bottle well filled. You could keep a chart of which birds come to visit the feeder. Draw each bird. A reference book will help you identify them.

Finding water is often difficult for animals and birds in winter, when streams and ponds may be frozen. A birdbath can help them out.

You may live in an area where it is very cold all winter. Then, you should wait for spring to build a birdbath. Birds can use it in the warmer seasons.

PROJECT

Make a birdbath

You will need
A garbage can lid
4 blocks of wood or bricks
Some water
A watering can

1. Chose a site out in the open for the birdbath. The birds must be able to see cats that come too close!

2. Place the blocks of wood in a square and balance the garbage can lid on top.

3. Fill the lid with water.

4. Check the bath every day. Fill it with clean water, and remove any ice that forms.

PEOPLE AND THE SEASONS

You may not realize it, but the seasons affect us every day of our lives. Just think about the clothes you wear and the food you eat. In summer you only need a few, light clothes. You drink cold drinks and eat salads and ice cream. As the weather gets colder in autumn, you need to wear more clothes. You want to eat hot food that warms you up.

It is fun to play in autumn leaves.

Our behavior also changes with the seasons. We spend much more time outdoors in the spring and summer months. We can play outdoor games and enjoy being in the yard, a field, the street, or a park.

We often go on vacation to places when the seasons are at their hottest or coldest. In summer, many people go to lakes, ponds, pools, or the ocean to cool off.

People go to places that have heavy snowfall in winter for skiing.

FARMING

Each season brings changes that affect the daily life and work of the farmer.

Farmers who grow crops have to get the land ready for planting in the winter. Autumn is when the fields are usually plowed.

Seed is sown in spring. Throughout the summer the crops have to be watered and sprayed against pests. The crops will be fully grown and ripe by the end of the summer. Now is the time to harvest them. It is important to get the harvest in before the weather turns bad. Heavy rains can flatten crops and ruin hay.

Farmers harvesting rye in Oregon.

On farms that raise animals, different events happen at different times of year. Just as in the wild, young animals are usually born in the spring. The weather has warmed up a bit, and the baby animals have a better chance of survival.

Sheep and cows spend the summer months grazing. Some will be taken to market at the end of the summer.

These sheep are able to survive winters outside. Their woolly coats keep them warm.

GLOSSARY

climate The usual weather of a place from year to year is called its climate.

equator An imaginary line around the middle of the earth. The equator is halfway between the North and South poles.

hemisphere Earth can be divided into two hemispheres, one north of and one south of the equator.

hibernation The period of inactivity that some animals go into during winter. A hibernating animal's body temperature is lowered and its breathing is slower. Hibernation is thought of as a deathlike state, but the animal is not dead. It is just staying alive during the harsh winter.

migration The movement of animals to find food or warmth as the seasons change.

photosynthesis The method by which plants make food using water, carbon dioxide, and sunlight.

pupa A stage in the life cycle of an insect. A pupa is when the insect is changing from a larva into an adult. It is protected by a covering, often a cocoon.

tropics The area around the equator, between the Tropic of Cancer and the Tropic of Capricorn.

FURTHER READING

Bryant-Mole, Karen. *Winter*. (Picture This! series). Heinemann Library, 1998.

Chapman, Gillian. *Spring*. (Seasonal Crafts series). Raintree Steck-Vaughn, 1998.

Ruiz, Andres L. *Seasons*. (Sequences of Earth & Space series). Sterling, 1996.

Schnur, Stephen. *Autumn: An Alphabet Acrostic*. Clarion Books, 1997.

Webster, David. *Summer.* (Exploring Nature Around the Year series). Silver Burdett Press, 1990.

The publishers would like to thank the following for permission to reproduce their pictures:

Bruce Coleman: page 4, 5 top, (Kim Taylor), 5 bottom, 14, (Tore Hagman), 16, (Kim Taylor), 17 top, 17 bottom, (Stephen J. Krasemann), 20, 21, (Gordon Langsbury), 23 top, (Jane Burton), 23 bottom (Stephen J. Krasemann), Cover; **Chris Fairclough**: page 10 inset, 22; **gettyone Stone**: page 8/9, (Arnulf Husmo), 12 top, (G. Bumgarner), 18 top, (R.K.G. Photography), 26, (Donna Day), 27 top (Andy Sacks), 27 bottom, (Jess Stock), 28 bottom, (Bruce Forster), 29, (John & Eliza Forder); **Oxford Scientific Films**: page 12 bottom, (John Gerlach), 18 bottom, (Terry Andrewartha), 20 bottom (Jim Clare), 28 top (David Curl); **Papilio Photographic**: page25.

INDEX